USING FACTA REMEDIES:

An FTC Staff Report on a Survey of Identity Theft Victims

March 2012 | Federal Trade Commission

Using FACTA Remedies

Contents

FTC Staff Report

INTRODUCTION

The Federal Trade Commission (FTC) maintains a longstanding and comprehensive program to combat identity theft. The FTC enforces a variety of laws requiring entities to protect consumer information and ensure that such information does not fall into the hands of identity thieves or other unauthorized persons. For example, the FTC enforces the Safeguards Rule under the Gramm-Leach Bliley Act;[1] the Fair Credit Reporting Act;[2] and the FTC Act's proscription against unfair and deceptive acts or practices[3] in cases where a business makes false or misleading claims about its data security procedures, or where its failure to employ reasonable security measures causes or is likely to cause substantial consumer injury that is not reasonably avoidable by consumers and not outweighed by countervailing benefits. Since 2001, the Commission has brought 35 law enforcement actions to ensure that businesses implement reasonable safeguards to protect the consumer information they maintain. In addition, the FTC manages the Identity Theft Clearinghouse, a secure online database of identity theft-related complaints, and analyzes this data to target consumer education efforts and assist criminal law enforcers.[4] The FTC also disseminates consumer education materials on identity theft, both directly and through public and private sector partners.

To further combat the problem of identity theft, in 2007, then-President Bush established an Identity Theft Task Force to craft a comprehensive national strategy. The Task Force issued a strategic plan, making over 30 recommendations for improving the federal identity theft

1. *See* 16 CFR Part 314, implementing 15 U.S.C. § 6801(b). The Federal Deposit Insurance Corporation, National Credit Union Administration, Securities and Exchange Commission, Office of the Comptroller of the Currency, Board of Governors of the Federal Reserve System, Office of Thrift Supervision, Secretary of the Treasury, and state insurance authorities have promulgated comparable safeguards requirements for the entities they regulate.

2. 15 U.S.C. §1681e (requires consumer reporting agencies to use reasonable procedures to ensure that entities to which they disclose consumer reports have a permissible purpose for receiving that information;) 15 U.S.C. § 1681w, and its implementing regulation, 16 C.F.R. Part 682 (imposes safe disposal obligations on entities that maintain consumer report information.).

3. 15 U.S.C. § 45(a).

4. *See e.g.,* FTC, *Consumer Sentinel Network Data Book for January - December, 2010* (Feb. 2011), *available at* http://ftc.gov/sentinel/reports/sentinel-annual-reports/sentinel-cy2010.pdf. The 2010 Data Book shows that over 250,000 consumers reported some form of identity theft, which represents 19% of the total number of complaints submitted to the Commission. This makes identity theft the most frequently reported category of consumer complaints, continuing a pattern that started over a decade ago.

strategy.[5] One of the recommendations was that the agencies involved in enforcing the Fair Credit Reporting Act (FCRA)[6] assess the impact and effectiveness of the rights established by Fair and Accurate Credit Transactions Act of 2003 (FACTA)[7] through the use of surveys. FACTA gives consumers the right to:

- place fraud alerts with the consumer reporting agencies (CRAs)[8];

- request a free credit report from each of the three national CRAs (Equifax, Experian, and TransUnion) when placing a fraud alert;

- block fraudulent information from appearing in their credit reports;

- receive a notice of these and other rights from the CRAs.

Accordingly, the FTC conducted a survey of consumers who had contacted the FTC to report that they were victims of identity theft.[9] The survey was designed to determine these consumers' general satisfaction with utilizing their FACTA rights and to examine the types of problems and issues they encountered while doing so. Because almost all of the FACTA rights involve the CRAs, which maintain consumer credit files, the survey focused largely on the victims' interactions with the CRAs.

This report summarizes the FTC staff's methodology in carrying out this survey, the results of the survey, and recommendations for further steps to assist consumers in utilizing their FACTA rights.

---

5. Combating Identity Theft: A Strategic Plan, The President's Identity Theft Task Force (2007), *available at* http://www.identitytheft.gov/reports/StrategicPlan.pdf.

6. Fair Credit Reporting Act, 15 U.S.C. § 1681 *et seq.* (1992).

7. Fair and Accurate Credit Transactions Act of 2003, Pub. L.No. 108-159, 117 Stat. 1952 (Dec. 4, 2003), codified at 15 U.S.C. § 1681 (2006).

8. The three nationwide CRAs that must comply with FACTA identity theft requirements are Experian, Equifax and TransUnion.

9. *See* Appendix I: Final Survey Instrument. The attached Survey Instrument also notes the responses received on each question.

METHODOLOGY

FTC staff designed a mail survey to be sent to 3,000 consumers who had contacted the FTC's hotline to report that they had become victims of identity theft.[10] Staff recognizes that the consumers who contacted the FTC may not be representative of victims of identity theft more generally and, for this reason, this survey is not designed to, and cannot be used to, extrapolate the overall experience of identity theft victims. This survey does, however, provide insight into the types of issues and problems that consumers may encounter in attempting to remedy the effects of identity theft.

To assist in the drafting of the survey, FTC staff used a contractor, ICF Macro, to conduct focus groups of identity theft victims to learn about their experiences utilizing their FACTA rights and to gain feedback on a draft version of the survey. In the fall of 2009, six focus groups consisting of a total of 52 people were convened in three cities, to discuss the participants' identity theft experience, their knowledge of their FACTA rights, their interactions with the CRAs, and their understanding and responses to the draft survey. The results of these focus group discussions were then used to revise the draft survey to improve usability and respondent comprehension, as well as to provide staff with additional insights into the experiences of victims of identity theft. A copy of the Focus Group Report is attached.[11]

The survey was then mailed to recipients with an explanatory cover letter, and recipients who had not yet responded were sent a reminder postcard two weeks after the survey was mailed. Ultimately, of the 3,000 surveys mailed, 634 were completed and returned, with the anonymity of the participants and their responses maintained throughout.

---

10. Over 250,000 consumers reported some form of identity theft, which represents 19% of the total number of complaints submitted to the Commission. This makes identity theft the most frequently reported category of consumer complaints, continuing a pattern that started over a decade ago. *See e.g.*, FTC, *Consumer Sentinel Network Data Book for January - December, 2010* (Feb. 2011), *available at* http://ftc.gov/sentinel/reports/sentinel-annual-reports/sentinel-cy2010.pdf.

11. *See* Appendix II: Macro Focus Group Report.

SUMMARY OF RESULTS

Respondents' Initial Contact with CRAs and Overall Satisfaction

Because almost all of the FACTA rights involve the CRAs, the survey first sought to determine whether the consumers had contacted the CRAs and, if so, their overall satisfaction with their experiences. Of the 634 respondents to the survey, 87% contacted one or more of the national CRAs as a result of becoming a victim of identity theft.[12] Fifty percent of respondents who contacted at least one CRA said that they contacted all three, while 28% contacted only one and 16% contacted two.[13] Although 34% of consumers who contacted the CRAs did so online, a large majority of these respondents (77%) also contacted the CRAs by telephone.[14] Most victims who contacted one or more CRAs by telephone attempted to speak to a representative rather than listen to a recording. Of those who attempted to speak to a representative, 81% eventually were able to do so. Sixty-one percent of those who spoke with a representative found it either very or somewhat easy to reach a representative, 36% found it either somewhat or very difficult, and 13% reported that it was very difficult.

The survey respondents who were able to reach a representative generally found the information they received helpful, with 77% stating that they found the information either somewhat or very useful. Only 20% responded that the information was only slightly or not at all useful.

These results echo the experiences reflected in the statements of many focus group participants. Most of the focus group participants contacted the CRAs by phone because they wanted to speak to a representative to discuss their problems. Some of the participants reported that it was difficult to reach a representative and complained that they spent too much time navigating automated menus and being placed on hold.

Most focus group participants also indicated that they did not have a clear understanding of their FACTA rights and did not have a clear plan for remedying their identity theft when they contacted the CRAs. Many of the participants indicated that they contacted the CRAs only to report the theft and to find out what actions they should take. In addition, many of the focus group participants were not aware that they should contact the CRAs until it was recommended to them by the FTC, a creditor, or police personnel.

---

12. An additional 11% said that they had not attempted to contact a CRA, while 2% said that they could not remember whether they had sought to contact a CRA.

13. Five percent indicated that they did not remember how many CRAs they had contacted.

14. Survey participants were permitted to indicate that they used multiple methods of contacting the CRAs. Thus, the responses to this question can total more than 100 percent.

The findings from the focus groups that many victims may not understand their rights and do not clearly understand what steps they should take to address identity theft is supported by the results of the survey. As discussed below, for most of the FACTA rights, a majority of respondents were not aware of the particular right before contacting the CRA, and in many cases appear to have exercised that right only after having been informed of it by the CRA.

Placing a Fraud Alert

One of the primary tools created by FACTA for actual and potential victims of identity theft is the fraud alert.[15] FACTA allows consumers who have a good faith suspicion that they have been, or are about to become, a victim of identity theft to place an initial fraud alert on their credit files.[16] Consumers need only request an alert with one of the nationwide CRAs, which in turn will notify the other two nationwide CRAs. Such alerts notify potential creditors that consumers may have been a victim of fraud and that special care should be taken to verify the consumers' identity before extending new credit.

Despite the advantages offered by fraud alerts, the survey showed that 44% of the respondents who contacted one or more CRAs were not aware before such contact of their right to place a fraud alert. Despite this initial lack of knowledge, 85% of respondents who contacted a CRA ultimately requested that a fraud alert be placed on their file.

Of the survey respondents who requested a fraud alert, 58% reported that all of the CRAs placed a fraud alert on their files. Six percent of those who asked that a fraud alert be placed on their records stated affirmatively that at least one CRA failed to place a fraud alert, while 36% were unsure whether all of the CRAs had placed alerts on their records.

Forty-four percent of respondents who requested a fraud alert stated that they were very satisfied with the process, and 32% reported being somewhat satisfied. Seventeen percent were either somewhat or very dissatisfied with the process. Of those survey respondents who specified a reason for their dissatisfaction with the process, the most common reason given related to questions about the effectiveness of the fraud alert, with some consumers stating that they were unsure if the fraud alert worked, and others affirmatively stating that it did not.

Staff notes that several focus group participants appeared to mistakenly believe that fraud alerts served as a sort of credit freeze, preventing potential creditors from accessing their credit

---

15. *See* 15 U.S.C. § 1681c-1.

16. An "initial fraud alert" stays on a consumer's credit report for 90 days. 15 U.S.C. § 1681c-1(a). Consumers can also request an "extended fraud alert," which stays on a consumer's report for 7 years. 15 U.S.C. § 1681c-1(b).

report at all, which may indicate that at least some victims who request fraud alerts do not fully understand the service they are requesting.[17]

Requesting a Free Credit Report When Placing a Fraud Alert

When a consumer places a fraud alert, he or she has a right to request a free credit report from each of the CRAs.[18] These credit reports are separate from, and in addition to, the annual free credit report that all consumers are entitled to receive from the three nationwide CRAs.[19] Half of survey respondents who contacted a CRA were unaware of this right prior to contacting the CRAs.[20] Nonetheless, 68% of respondents who contacted a CRA requested a free credit report after placing their fraud alerts.[21] The majority of respondents (56%) who requested a free credit report requested it by telephone, 33% used a website, 14% mailed a form, and 13% wrote to the CRA.[22]

The survey results reflect some difficulties with consumers' requests for credit reports being fulfilled. Of those who requested a free credit report, only 51% stated that they received it from all of the CRAs they contacted, while 33% stated that they received it from only some of the CRAs they contacted, and 11% stated that they did not receive any credit reports. In addition, several focus group participants complained that they had to wait weeks or even months before receiving their requested report. In at least one instance, a participant did not receive the credit report until after the 90-day fraud alert had expired.

Despite these issues, 43% of respondents stated that they were very satisfied with the process of requesting the free credit reports after placing a fraud alert and 32% stated that they were somewhat satisfied. Twenty-two percent of the respondents reported being either somewhat or very dissatisfied, however, with the most common reason given being a failure to receive one or

---

17. For example, one survey respondent was dissatisfied because new credit cards with new account numbers were still issued to the identity thief.

18. *See* 15 U.S.C. § 1681j (d).

19. *See* 15 U.S.C. § 1681j(a)(1); 16 C.F.R. 610 (requires each nationwide CRA - Experian, Equifax, and Trans Union - to provide consumers, upon request, a free copy of their credit report once every 12 months).

20. Forty-seven percent of respondents who contacted a CRA said that they were aware that they could request a free copy of their credit report when placing a fraud alert, while 3% said that they did not know whether or not they were aware.

21. It should be noted, however, that during the focus group several participants confused their right to a free credit report when requesting a fraud alert with their right to a free annual credit report. Although steps were taken to clarify this distinction in the final survey, it is possible that some respondents thatwho reported obtaining this free credit report were actually obtainedreferring only to a free annual report.

22. Respondents were permitted to indicate that they had used multiple means to request copies of their reports. The sum of the responses therefore total to more than 100 percent.

more of the free credit reports. Another common complaint was the difficulty of the process, with one respondent stating that "[t]he system doesn't confirm if you have been successful ordering your reports and is difficult to use."

In addition, several consumers in the focus groups complained that they felt pushed into paying for additional services while placing their fraud alert. One complained that when attempting to obtain a credit report, the respondent was charged "for [a] monthly credit report using this site."

Disputing the Accuracy of Information on Credit Reports

Consumers have a right to dispute the accuracy of information on their credit reports.[23] They may dispute the information either with the creditor that provided the information to the CRAs or with the CRAs themselves.[24] When a creditor or a CRA receives a dispute, it is required to perform a reasonable investigation to determine whether the contested information is accurate. If the information is inaccurate, the report must be corrected.

A majority of respondents (60%) who contacted a CRA were aware before such contact that they had the right to challenge the accuracy of information on their credit report. Thirty-six percent of respondents who contacted a CRA disputed the accuracy of information on their credit report in connection with the identity theft that led to the contact. Of those who did dispute information, 72% filed disputes with a CRA, while 46% contacted the creditor that provided the information to the CRA. Respondents filed disputes about many different types of information: 47% challenged identification and employment information, 48% disputed payment information related to a particular debt, and 40% complained of unauthorized creditors obtaining their report.[25]

Of those respondents who disputed information, 52% reported that the information was corrected or removed. Twenty-nine percent stated that the information was not corrected, and 18% said that they were not sure. It should be noted that this survey made no attempt to assess the merits of the respondents' disputes, so there is no way to determine if the challenged information should have

---

23. *See* 15 U.S.C. § 1681i.

24. Although FACTA, Pub. L. No. 108-159, 117 Stat. 1952 (Dec. 4, 2003), codified at 15 U.S.C. § 1681 (2006), gives consumers the right to dispute their information accuracy directly with the furnishers of the information, at the time the survey was conducted, the rule for reporting of disputes directly to furnishers had not yet gone into effect. The rule, issued jointly by the FTC, the Federal Reserve, the Federal Deposit Insurance Corporation, the National Credit Union Administration, the Office of the Comptroller of the Currency, and the Office of Thrift Supervision, went into effect on July 1, 2010. 16 C.F.R. Part 660.4.

25. Survey participants were permitted to indicate that they had disputed information with more than one type of entity and also that they had disputed multiple types of information.

been corrected or not. In some instances the disputed information may have been correct or the respondent may not have properly disputed the information.[26]

Of those respondents who had information corrected by the CRA, most reported that it was corrected relatively easily, with 42% doing so after a single contact and 27% needing two contacts. Twenty-four percent, however, required three to five contacts, and 4% were required to contact the CRA six or more times. Overall, 57% of respondents who challenged information on their credit report were either very or somewhat satisfied with the process of correcting that information.[27] Seventeen percent of respondents reported being somewhat dissatisfied and 21% being very dissatisfied. This was the highest percentage of dissatisfaction expressed concerning the FACTA rights addressed by this survey. For those respondents who gave a reason for their dissatisfaction, the most common reason given was dissatisfaction with the result of the dispute. Again, the survey does not provide any insight into the merits of the disputes, so it is possible that some of these dissatisfied respondents may not have been entitled to a different outcome. For example, several focus group respondents did not understand that a CRA needed to investigate their dispute and believed that the information should have been removed immediately. Similar misunderstandings may have raised the level of dissatisfaction among survey respondents.

In addition to the complaints about the outcome of disputes, several survey respondents complained about the difficulty and length of the dispute process. One survey respondent reported that "[i]t took several certified letters to get resolved," while another complained that "[i]f your identity is stolen it becomes a full time job to get it fixed. Everybody, credit cards, banks, CRA wants [sic] to pass the buck."

26. FTC staff is currently conducting a series of studies to examine the accuracy and completeness of information in consumers' credit reports. Staff has conducted two pilot studies to date, and is currently conducting a nationwide survey based on a nationally representative sample. *See Report to Congress Under Section 319 of the Fair and Accurate Credit Transactions Act of 2003, Fed. Trade Comm'n.,* Dec. 2010, *available at* http://www.ftc.gov/os/2010/12/101230factarpt.pdf.

27. Not surprisingly, those who were successful in getting the disputed information removed from their reports were more satisfied that those who were unsuccessful. Only 6% of those who failed to get the disputed information removed indicated that they were either very satisfied or somewhat satisfied with their experience, while 83% of those who had the information removed indicated that they were very or somewhat satisfied. Similarly, those who needed fewer contacts to get the information removed were more likely to be satisfied. Of those who had the information removed after one or two contacts with a CRA, 94% indicated that they were very or somewhat satisfied. Among those who required three or more contacts before getting the information removed, the level of satisfaction fell to 57%.

Blocking the Release of Fraudulent Information in Credit Reports

Generally, if a consumer identifies information on his or her credit report as being the result of identity theft and provides a copy of an identity theft report[28] to the CRA, FACTA requires the CRA to block the reporting of that information.[29] The right to block information is distinct from the right to dispute information. A block is specifically aimed at information that is the result of identity theft and permanently prevents the reporting of the information to persons or companies requesting credit report information. The CRA is required to effectuate this request within four days of receiving it. If a CRA receives a valid request to block information accompanied by an identity theft report, then the CRA may not report the blocked information unless it reasonably determines that the block was made in error or was based on a material misrepresentation by the consumer. The CRA must also notify the furnisher of the information that the information may be the result of identity theft and has been blocked.

Seventy-eight percent of respondents who contacted a CRA were not aware of the right to block information prior to contacting the CRA. Further, in the focus groups, participants had difficulty understanding this right even after the moderator explained it to them, with many continuing to confuse it with the rights to dispute information or to place a fraud alert. It is unsurprising, then, that very few respondents who contacted a CRA attempted to exercise this right - only 21% attempted to block the reporting of information resulting from identity theft. Of those who requested that information be blocked, 46% reported that all of the CRAs blocked the information, while 18% stated that only some of the CRAs did so and 9% reported that none of the CRAs did so.[30] As with the dispute process, the survey was not designed to assess the merits of the respondents' requests for blocking, so it is not possible to determine how many of the attempts to block should have been granted. It is possible that some of the requests were appropriately denied, either because the information was not a result of identity theft or because the respondent failed to provide an identity theft report.

28. An identity theft report is defined as an official report filed with a law enforcement agency, the filing of which subjects the consumer to criminal penalties if the information is false. *See* 15 U.S.C. § 1681a(q)(4).
29. *See* 15 U.S.C. § 1681c-2.
30. Twenty-five percent said that they did not know whether or not their information was blocked.

Sixty-four percent of respondents were either somewhat or very satisfied with the process of blocking information on their reports. Twenty-four percent of respondents stated that they were either somewhat or very dissatisfied.[31]

Notice of Rights

FACTA requires the CRAs to send a notice of consumer rights to any consumer who contacts them to report a belief that the consumer is a victim of fraud or identity theft.[32] The notice must contain a summary of the rights available to consumers with respect to remedying the effects of identity theft and information on how to contact the FTC for more information.[33] Over 45% of the respondents reported that they had received a notice from at least one of the CRAs they contacted. Twenty-seven percent of respondents who contacted a CRA reported that they had not received a notice from any of the CRAs, and an additional 28% stated that they were not sure if they had received such a notice.

Overall Satisfaction

The survey showed that 68% of the respondents were somewhat or very satisfied with their overall experiences with the CRAs. Twenty-five percent, however, were somewhat or very dissatisfied. There are several recurring themes to the reasons for this dissatisfaction.

The most common reason given was the difficulty in reaching a representative when contacting the CRAs. One respondent stated that "[i]t was not possible to speak to a live person. The automated system is very confusing and does not confirm that what you have attempted is being accomplished." Another said that "I still have not been able to get ahold [sic] of anyone. They want you to send a lot of information in and I don't feel comfortable doing that (with already having my identity stolen.)" In addition, other respondents reported frustration because they believed that the CRAs did not have sympathy for their plight and sometimes treated them with suspicion. For example, one respondent said that "[s]ince the person had all of my personal information I was treated more like a criminal than a victim and it was very hard to prove I was myself." Likewise, one focus group participant said that the CRAs made him feel like "suspect number one."

---

31. Again, success is associated with satisfaction. Of those who said that their information was blocked by all of the CRAs, 92% indicated that they were either very or somewhat satisfied with the process. On the other hand, all of those who reported that their information was not blocked by any of the CRAs reported that they were very dissatisfied with the process.

32. *See* 15 U.S.C. § 1681g (d).

33. *See id.;* 16 C.F.R. Part 698, App. E (model summary of rights).

Another frequent complaint was that the overall process for remedying identity theft was too difficult. Respondents said that the process took too long and placed too much of the burden on them. For instance, one respondent complained that "[i]t was easier for the thief to change my info on my credit report than it has been for me to change it back. Still not right after working to fix it for six months." Another stated that "I feel that I shouldn't have had to do all the leg work and one call or email should have been enough during this stressful time."

Many of the dissatisfied respondents were upset that their problems had not been adequately resolved. These respondents generally reported that the incorrect information remained on their credit reports after multiple attempts to have it removed. One said that "[t]hey keep sending me reports that still contain accounts that do not belong to me. There are late charges that might affect my credit rating." Another reported that "I have tried and tried to get wrong information corrected or taken off and haven't been able to."

Also notable was the fact that several respondents reported that they had felt pressured into paying for additional services when seeking help from the CRAs. One respondent stated that "[t]hey kept trying to sell me a fraud alert package and I often had to ask to speak to a manager to get them to put a freeze on my credit reports." Likewise, others complained that "[t]hey tried to sell me fraud prevention products" and that it was "very difficult to avoid marketing strategies of CRAs for services." Several focus group participants also complained that while attempting to place a fraud alert, they were sold various identity theft prevention products.

These complaints indicate that at least some identity theft victims experience problems dealing with CRAs and understanding their FACTA rights. Although this survey does not demonstrate how common these problems are with identity theft victims in general, it does show that the problems arise and can be frustrating to victims who are already struggling with the impact of identity theft on their lives.

CONCLUSION

Despite the 68% general satisfaction rate with the CRAs, the survey reveals three areas where respondents faced difficulties in exercising their FACTA rights. First, one prominent complaint was the difficulty in reaching a representative at a CRA with whom to speak about identity theft. Many respondents said that it was difficult or impossible to move past the automated response system and reach a representative. Given that nearly three-quarters of the respondents who contacted a CRA attempted to reach a representative, the survey responses suggest that CRAs may need to do more to make it easier for identity theft victims to speak to a representative.

Second, the survey results suggest that a relatively small number of identity theft victims are aware of their FACTA rights. Less than half of the respondents were aware of most of their rights prior to contacting the CRAs. Even for the most well-understood right – disputing inaccurate information – only 60% of respondents who contacted a CRA were aware of this right prior to contacting the CRA. Accordingly, the FTC, other federal and state agencies, and the CRAs should do more to educate the public about their rights.

Indeed, the overall results highlight the importance of ongoing consumer education efforts of government agencies and the CRAs. At the Commission, consumer education about identity theft continues to be an important priority. The Commission has an extensive program to provide consumers with the knowledge and tools needed to protect themselves from identity theft and to deal with its consequences.[34]

As one of the primary sources of information for consumers, the CRAs also play an important and continuing role in informing identity theft victims about their FACTA rights. Congress recognized this important role by requiring the CRAs to provide victims with a summary of consumer identity theft rights.[35] To that end, the Commission has prepared a model summary of rights, which is available at 16 C.F.R. Part 698, Appendix E.

Notwithstanding the consumer education efforts of both the Commission and the CRAs, consumers continue to experience difficulties understanding their FACTA rights. Both the Commission and the CRAs should improve and better target their consumer education and outreach programs to address FACTA rights for consumers who are victims of identity theft.

Third, both the survey respondents and the focus groups raised concerns about the CRAs using consumer contacts about identity theft as an opportunity to sell identity theft protection products. Several respondents and focus group participants complained that they felt pressured to buy one or more products and that, in some cases, they received services that they did not want or need. Given these incidents, the Consumer Financial Protection Bureau, which has examination and rulemaking authority in this area, may want to address these practices. In addition, to the extent

---

34. The Commission makes available a wide variety of consumer educational materials to help consumers deter, detect, and defend against identity theft. For example, the Commission publishes a victim recovery guide – *Takinging Charge: What to do if Your Identity is Stolen* – that explains the immediate steps identity theft victims should take to address the crime; how to obtain a credit report and correct fraudulent information in credit reports; how to file a police report; and how to protect personal information. The Commission has distributed over 3.8 million copies of the recovery guide and has recorded over 3.5 million visits to the Web version. The guide is available at www.ftc.gov/bcp/ed/pubs/consumers/idtheft/idt04.pdf.

35. 15 U.S.C. § 1681g(c).

any marketing of identity theft protection products involves unfair or deceptive practices, the Commission retains authority to bring enforcement actions to protect against such conduct.[36]

These concerns are consistent with the ones recently addressed in the context of the amendments to the Free Annual File Disclosures Rule.[37] Under the amended Rule, nationwide CRAs must delay advertising products and services when a consumer attempts to get a free annual credit report through www.annualcreditreport.com – the only authorized source for free annual credit reports – until after the consumer receives their free report.[38] Going forward, consumers should be able to obtain their free annual credit reports through www.annualcreditreport.com without the distraction of advertising for monitoring or other product or service advertisements.

Given the difficult and stressful position of identity theft victims, every step should be taken to ensure that the tools available to remedy the effects of identity theft are as simple and easy to use as possible.

36. *See FTC v. Consumerinfo.com, Inc.*, SACV05-801AHS(MLGx) (C.D. Cal. Aug. 15, 2005); *FTC v. Consumerinfo.com, Inc.,* SACV05-801AHS(MLGx) (C.D. Cal. Jan. 8, 2007). In the original case in 2005, the Commission charged, among other things, that defendant Consumerinfo.com, an affiliate of the nationwide CRA Experian, had deceptively mimicked the FACT Act free annual report program. The stipulated order required the defendant to make prominent disclosures that its program is not associated with the free annual report program and provide a link to the official website for that program, www.annualcreditreport.com. The defendants also agreed to pay $950,000 in disgorgement, and to provide refunds to dissatisfied past customers. In the 2007 case, the Commission alleged that Consumerinfo.com had violated the 2005 order. The new order includes a $300,000 judgment for consumer redress.

37. 16 C.F.R. Part 610.

38. 75 Fed.Reg. 9726 (March 3, 2010); 16 C.F.R Part 610.

Appendix I
Annotated Identity Theft Victim Survey

OMB No. 3084-0153
Expires: July 31, 2012

Disclosure of Estimated Burden

The estimated average burden associated with this information collection is 8 minutes per respondent. Burden estimates include the time for reviewing instructions, gathering and maintaining data in the required form, and completing the information collection, but exclude the time for compiling and maintaining bsiness records in the normal course of a respondent's activities. A Federal agency may not conduct or sponsor, and an organization (or a person) is not required to respond to a collection of information, unless it displays a currently valid OMB control number. Comments concerning the accuracy of this burden estimate and suggestions for reducing this burden should be directed to the Office of Information and Regulatory Affairs, Office of Management and Budget, Washington, D.C. 20503, and to Anthony Rodriguez, Federal Trade Commission, 600 Pennsylvania Avenue, N.W., Mail Stop NJ-3158, Washington, D.C. 20580.

FTC IDENTITY THEFT VICTIM SURVEY

This survey includes questions relating to your experience as a victim of identity theft and your interactions with one or more credit bureaus. Please respond as accurately and completely as possible.

Section 1: Initial Contact with Credit Bureaus

1. Did you try to contact one or more credit reporting companies (also known as credit bureaus) such as Experian, Equifax, or TransUnion as a result of discovering you were a victim of identity theft? **(Check one answer)**

    86.6% Yes
    11.2% No ➜ **SKIP to Question 32**
    2.1%   Don't remember or not sure ➜ **SKIP to Question 32**
    Obs=634

1a. When did you first contact one or more credit bureau(s)?

    5.3%   Less than one month ago
    78.5% 1-6 month(s) ago
    9.0%   6-12 months ago
    6.4%   More than 1 year ago
    Obs=545

2. How many credit bureaus did you contact? **(Check one answer)**

    28.1% One
    15.5% Two
    50.2% Three or more
    5.5%   Don't remember or not sure
    Obs=548

3. How did you contact the credit bureau(s)? **(Check as many as apply)**

    76.5% Phone
    19.3% Mail
    34.2% Online

4.2%   Other ➔ Please explain: _____
1.6%   Don't remember or not sure
Obs=549

4.   Did you try to speak with a live person at one or more credit bureaus? **(Check one answer)**

    74.4% Yes
    21.6% No ➔ **SKIP to Question 8**
    3.8%   Don't remember or not sure ➔ **SKIP to Question 8**
    Obs=547

5.   Were you able to speak with a live person? **(Check one answer)**

    80.7% Yes
    17.1% No ➔ **SKIP to Question 8**
    1.5%   Don't remember or not sure ➔ **SKIP to Question 8**
    Obs=410

6.   In general, how easy or difficult was it to reach a live person? **(Check one answer)**

    24.8% Very easy
    35.8% Somewhat easy   Combined Easy: 60.6%
    23.6% Somewhat difficult
    12.5% Very difficult   Combined Difficult: 36.1%
    2.4%   Don't remember or not sure
    Obs=335

7.   Overall, how useful was the information you received when you spoke to a live person? **(Check one answer)**

    45.7% Very useful
    31.6% Somewhat useful
    14.3% Only slightly useful
    6.0%   Not at all useful
    1.8%   Don't remember or not sure
    Obs = 335

8.   Overall, how satisfied were you with your experience with the credit bureau(s)? **(Check one answer)**

    30.4% Very satisfied
    38.1% Somewhat satisfied   Combined Satisfied: 68.5%
    13.9% Somewhat dissatisfied
    14.1% Very dissatisfied   Combined Dissatisfied: 28.0%
    3.5%   Don't know or not sure
    Obs=546

8a. Again, thinking of your overall experience with the credit bureau(s), please tell us why you felt satisfied or dissatisfied with your experience:

_____

_____

Section 2: Placing a Fraud Alert

DEFINITION: Placing a fraud alert on your credit report requires creditors to follow certain procedures to verify your identity before issuing credit in your name. Often, this means that when a business wants to open a new account in your name, they will first contact you to get your permission to open the account.

9. **Before you contacted a credit bureau,** were you aware that you had a right to request a fraud alert if you believed that you were, or were likely to become, a victim of identity theft? **(Check one answer)**

   50.2%   Yes
   44.3%   No
   5.1%   Don't remember or not sure
   Obs=548

10. Did you ask one or more credit bureaus to place a fraud alert on your credit report? **(Check one answer)**

    84.8%   Yes
    10.8%   No ➔ **SKIP to Question 19**
    3.3%   Don't remember or not sure ➔ **SKIP to Question 19**
    Obs=548

11. Did you ask for an initial (90 day) fraud alert, an extended (7 year) fraud alert, or both? **(Check one answer)**

    57.7%   Initial alert only
    4.3%   Extended alert only
    22.8%   Both initial and extended alerts
    13.5%   Don't remember or not sure
    Obs=466

12. To the best of your knowledge, was a fraud alert actually placed on your credit report? **(Check one answer)**

    58.4%   All of the bureaus placed a fraud alert
    5.6%   Some of the bureaus placed a fraud alert, others did not
    17.6%   Some of the bureaus placed a fraud alert, I don't know about others
    18.0%   Don't remember or not sure
    Obs=466

13. Overall, how satisfied were you with the experience of placing a fraud alert on your credit report? **(Check one answer)**

    44.1%   Very satisfied
    32.0%   Somewhat satisfied   Combined Satisfied: 76.1%
    10.5%   Somewhat dissatisfied
    6.2%   Very dissatisfied   Combined Dissatisfied: 16.6%

6.8%   Don't know or not sure
Obs=469

13a. Please tell us why you felt satisfied or dissatisfied with the experience of placing a fraud alert:

_____

_____

_____

Section 3: Requesting a Free Credit Report

DEFINITION: When you place a fraud alert on your credit report, you have the right to request a free credit report from each of the credit bureaus. This is separate from your right to an annual free credit report.

NOTE: If you did not answer "Yes" to Question 10, please skip to Question 19 and do not answer this section.

14. **Before you contacted a credit bureau,** were you aware that you had this right to request a free credit report when you place a fraud alert? **(Check one answer)**

46.7% Yes
50.0% No
3.3%   Don't remember or not sure
Obs=454

15. Did you request a free copy of your credit report from one or more credit bureaus after you placed a fraud alert?

68.0% Yes
26.9% No ➜ **SKIP to Question 19**
5.1%   Don't remember or not sure ➜ **SKIP to Question 19**
Obs=453

16. How did you ask for a free copy of your credit report from the credit bureau(s)? **(Check as many as apply)**

56.2% Call
12.7% Write
13.6% Mail a form
32.5% Go to the website ➜ **If you recall, please identify website:** _____
4.2%   Do something else ➜ **Please explain:** _____
3.6%   Don't remember or not sure
Obs=308

17. Did you receive a free copy of your credit report from the credit bureau(s)?

    50.8% I received a free copy of my credit report from all of the bureaus I contacted
    32.9% I received a free copy of my credit report from some of the bureaus I contacted
    11.4% I did not receive a copy of my credit report from any of the bureaus I contacted
    3.9% Don't remember or not sure
    Obs=307

18. Overall, how satisfied were you with your experience in getting your free credit report from the credit bureau(s)? **(Check one answer)**

    43.1% Very satisfied
    31.5% Somewhat satisfied   Combined Satisfied: 74.5%
    10.6% Somewhat dissatisfied
    11.3% Very dissatisfied   Combined Dissatisfied: 21.9%
    3.3% Don't know or not sure
    Obs=302

18a. Please tell us why you felt satisfied or dissatisfied with your experience in getting a free credit report:

_____

_____

_____

_____

Section 4: Disputing the Accuracy of Information in Your Credit Report

DEFINITION: You have the right to dispute the accuracy of information in your credit report that you believe is inaccurate. The credit bureau will investigate your dispute with the company that reported the disputed information. If the information is, in fact, inaccurate, you have the right to have it corrected or removed.

19. Before you contacted a credit bureau, were you aware that you had this right to dispute the accuracy of information in your credit report? **(Check one answer)**

    60.3% Yes
    34.4% No
    5.2% Don't remember or not sure
        Obs=541

20. Did you dispute the accuracy of any identity theft-related information in your credit report? **(Check one answer)**

   36.2% Yes
   56.6% No ➜ **SKIP to Question 26**
   7.0%   Don't remember or not sure ➜ **SKIP to Question 26**

21. With whom did you file your dispute? **(Check as many as apply)**

   71.7% One or more of the credit bureaus (Experian, Equifax, or TransUnion)
   46.1% The company that appeared on your credit report with the account or information you were disputing
   17.3% Other ➜ **Please explain:** _____
   2.1%   Don't remember or not sure
   Obs=191

22. What information in your credit report did you dispute? **(Check all that apply)**

   46.6% Identification and employment information (name, address, employer, etc.)
   48.2% Payment information related to a particular debt (account, amount owed, etc.)
   39.8% Creditors you did not authorize to obtain your report
   24.1% Other ➜ **Please elaborate:** _____
   4.7%   Don't remember or not sure
   Obs=191

23. Was the information you disputed removed or corrected? **(Check one answer)**

   52.4% Yes
   28.8% No ➜ **SKIP to Question 25**
   17.8% Don't remember or not sure ➜ **SKIP to Question 25**
   Obs=191

24. If you contacted the credit bureau(s) to file your dispute, how many times did you contact the credit bureau(s) before the information you disputed was removed or corrected? **(Check one answer)**

   42.2% Once
   26.5% Twice
   23.5% Three to five times
   3.9%   Six times or more
   2.0%   Don't remember or not sure
   Obs=102

25. Overall, how satisfied were you with your experience in disputing information in your credit report? **(Check one answer)**

   28.7% Very satisfied
   28.7% Somewhat satisfied   Combined Satisfied: 57.4%
   16.5% Somewhat dissatisfied
   21.3% Very dissatisfied   Combined Dissatisfied: 37.8%
   4.3%   Don't know or not sure
   Obs=188

25a. Please tell us why you felt satisfied or dissatisfied with your experience in disputing information in your credit report:

_____

_____

_____

_____

Section 5: Blocking the Release of Fraudulent Information in Your Credit Report

DEFINITION: You have the right to block the release of fraudulent information in your credit report that is the result of identity theft. This right is different than your right to place a fraud alert on your account, or your right to dispute inaccurate information on your credit report.

26. **Before you contacted a credit bureau,** were you aware that you had this right to block fraudulent information in your credit report from being released to others? **(Check one answer)**

   18.2% Yes
   77.8% No
   3.9%   Don't remember or not sure
   Obs=544

27. Did you ask one or more credit bureaus to block fraudulent identity theft-related information in your credit report from being released? **(Check one answer)**

   21.3% Yes
   66.1% No **➔ SKIP to Question 31**
   12.4% Don't remember or not sure **➔ SKIP to Question 31**
   Obs=539

28. To the best of your knowledge, did the bureaus you asked actually block fraudulent identity theft-related information in your credit report from being released? **(Check one answer)**

   45.5% All of the bureaus blocked the information
   17.9% Only some of the bureaus blocked the information
   8.9%   None of the bureaus blocked the information **➔ SKIP to Question 30**
   25.0% Don't remember or not sure **➔ SKIP to Question 30**
   Obs=112

29. How long did it typically take the credit bureaus to block information in your credit report? **(Check one answer)**

   17.6% One day (24 hours)

35.1% 2 - 7 days
17.6% More than 7 days
28.4% Don't remember or not sure
Obs=74

30. Overall, how satisfied were you with your experience in blocking fraudulent information in your credit report? (**Check one answer**)

29.5% Very satisfied
34.8% Somewhat satisfied   Combined Satisfied: 64.3%
8.9%   Somewhat dissatisfied
15.2% Very dissatisfied   Combined Dissatisfied: 24.1%
11.6% Don't know or not sure
Obs=112

30a. Please tell us why you felt satisfied or dissatisfied with your experience in blocking information in your credit report:

_____

_____

_____

_____

Section 6: Additional Questions

31. By law, credit bureaus must give you a notice that summarizes your rights as a victim of identity theft. Did you receive such a "notice of rights" from the credit bureau(s) you contacted? (**Check one answer**)

    32.7% I received a "notice of rights" from all of the credit bureaus I contacted
    12.7% I received a "notice of rights" from some of the credit bureaus I contacted
    26.7% I did not receive a "notice of rights" from any of the credit bureaus I contacted
    27.6% I don't remember or not sure
    Obs=536

32. Feel free to include additional comments below:

    _____

    _____

    _____

    _____

Thank you for completing this survey, please return in enclosed postage-paid envelope.

Appendix II
Focus Group Report

Final Report

Assessment of Fair and Accurate Transactions Act (FACT Act) Remedies Under the FCRA— Consumer Focus Groups

SUBMITTED TO:

Federal Trade Commission
600 Pennsylvania Avenue, NW
Washington, DC 20580

SUBMITTED BY:

an ICF International Company

11785 Beltsville Drive
Calverton, Maryland 20705

APRIL 2010

TABLE OF CONTENTS

Appendix A: Identity Theft Victim Survey

Appendix B: Focus Group Moderator Guides

Appendix C: Focus Group Recruitment Letter

Appendix D: Participant Recruitment Screener

INTRODUCTION

The Fair and Accurate Credit Transactions Act (FACT Act), which was enacted by Congress in 2003, amended the Fair Credit Reporting Act. A primary goal of the FACT Act was to help consumers fight the growing crime of identity theft. To this end, the FACT Act provided a number of new remedies for actual or potential victims of identity theft. These remedies included the rights for consumers to do the following:

- Place fraud alerts on their credit file;

- Request a free credit report from each of the national credit reporting agencies (CRAs)— Experian, TransUnion, and Equifax—when placing a fraud alert;

- Dispute the accuracy of information in their credit file;

- Block the release of fraudulent information in their credit report.

To examine consumers' experiences with CRAs when trying to exercise one or more of their FACT Act remedies, the Federal Trade Commission (FTC) contracted with ICF Macro to conduct a series of focus groups with victims of identity theft across the country who had previously contacted the FTC. The study was also designed to gather feedback on a draft version of the Identity Theft Victim Survey, a mail survey that the FTC intends to conduct among victims of identity theft to learn about their interactions with the CRAs. The FTC plans to use the data gathered through this research to inform and guide future enforcement and education efforts.

This report provides a summary of ICF Macro's methodology in carrying out these focus groups, as well as an overview of key findings from the study.

METHODOLOGY

Structure of Focus Groups

The focus groups were convened in Washington, DC (September 23, 2009); Chicago, IL (October 20, 2009); and Los Angeles, CA (October 22, 2009). These locations were selected so that data would be collected from three geographically dispersed locations.

Two focus groups were held in each of the three locations. One focus group, which lasted 90 minutes, consisted of a structured discussion that gave participants an opportunity to discuss topics such as the nature of their contacts with the CRAs; their motivations for contacting them; and the factors that influenced their level of satisfaction with the CRAs. A significant part of the discussion focused on how well participants understood each of the FACT Act remedies.

The second of the two focus groups lasted for two hours and had an additional component. The purpose of these longer focus groups was not only to understand participants' interactions with the CRAs, but also to pilot and gather feedback on the draft Identity Theft Victim Survey. During the first 30 minutes of these focus groups, participants completed the Identity Theft Victim Survey. They then participated in a discussion in which they talked about their interactions with the CRAs and provided additional feedback on the survey. The survey that participants completed is provided as Appendix A; moderator guides for both groups are provided in Appendix B.[1]

Recruitment

Participants for the focus groups were recruited from a list provided by the FTC. This list consisted of a sample of consumers that had filed a complaint with the FTC relating to identity theft. A random sample of 780 people with mailing addresses and telephone numbers was selected to be targeted for recruitment in each city.

As the first step in the recruiting process, the FTC sent a letter of invitation to consumers in the sample (Appendix C). The letter indicated that the FTC was holding focus groups and provided consumers with a toll-free telephone number to contact if they were interested in participating. Several days after the FTC sent the letters, recruiters followed up with potential participants by telephone. Recruiters screened potential participants on several criteria using a structured screening protocol (Appendix D). This screener ensured that all participants had suffered an identity theft within the past year, and that they had subsequently contacted one or more CRAs as a result. Participants were also screened on other demographic variables such as age, ethnicity, and education level in order to ensure diverse representation in the groups.

There were a total of 52 participants in the focus groups. As shown in Table 1, these participants varied in terms of gender, age, ethnicity, and educational level.

Table 1: Demographic Characteristics of Focus Group Participants

Total Participants	19	20	13	52
Gender				
Male	9 (47%)	9 (45%)	6 (46%)	24 (46%)
Female	10 (53%)	11 (55%)	7 (54%)	28 (54%)
Age				
18–34	3 (16%)	8 (40%)	4 (31%)	15 (29%)
35–54	8 (42%)	9 (45%)	6 (46%)	23 (44%)
55+	8 (42%)	3 (15%)	3 (23%)	14 (27%)

[1] Both the survey and the moderator guides were revised slightly between the Washington, DC and Chicago, IL focus groups; the versions provided as appendices are those that were used in Chicago and Los Angeles.

	Ethnicity			
African American	13 (68%)	10 (50%)	5 (38%)	28 (54%)
Caucasian	4 (21%)	6 (30%)	5 (38%)	15 (29%)
Hispanic	2 (11%)	3 (15%)	3 (23%)	8 (15%)
American Indian	-	1 (5%)	-	1 (2%)
	Education Level			
Less than high school	-	1 (5%)	-	1 (2%)
High school graduate	4 (21%)	6 (30%)	3 (23%)	13 (25%)
Some college	6 (32%)	7 (35%)	6 (46%)	19 (37%)
College graduate or higher	9 (47%)	6 (30%)	4 (31%)	19 (37%)

Note: Due to rounding, some percentages may not total 100 percent.

Participants in the focus groups were at various stages of interacting with the CRAs. In some cases, CRAs had already taken the actions requested by participants, or their identity theft had been resolved. Others were still in the process of working with the CRAs to get a credit report or to remove inaccurate information from their credit reports.

SUMMARY OF RESEARCH FINDINGS

Participants' Experience Interacting with CRAs

First Reactions to Identity Theft

- When asked what they did when they first found out that their identity was stolen, some participants said that at first they did not know what to do. A few participants said that the first thing they did was to do an online search for information on what to do if your identity is stolen.

- Many of the participants contacted the business or institution with which their identity was misused, such as the IRS, their bank, their credit card company, or a specific store or business. Many also contacted the police and the FTC. For many, it was only after contacting these other organizations that they learned they should contact a CRA about their identity theft.

Reasons for Contacting the CRAs

- Before their identity theft, participants generally had little awareness of their FACT Act rights, and many were not clear about the role of a CRA in resolving their identity theft. One person commented, "It doesn't occur to people that the credit bureaus have any responsibility for this kind of identity theft. They may be the first line of defense but I don't think the public is aware of that."

- In most cases when participants contacted the CRAs, they were not sure of the specific actions they needed to take. Only a few participants knew in advance to contact the CRAs for specific actions, like placing a fraud alert. Many participants said they called the CRAs to let them know about their identity theft and to find out what actions they should take. In those cases, the CRAs informed the victim of what they needed to do and the steps needed to do it.

- After their identity theft, most participants initially did not contact a CRA specifically to access their FACT Act rights because they were not aware of them. For most participants, the major reasons for contacting a CRA was to document their identity theft, clear up their credit, attempt to mitigate the impact of the identity theft, or find out who was responsible for stealing their identity.

- Participants learned that they should contact the CRAs from a variety of sources. In many cases, participants were told to contact the CRAs from one of the other entities that they alerted to their identity theft, such as their bank or the police. One said that she knew to contact the CRAs from information on free annual credit reports that she requested each year. As noted above, a few learned that they should contact the CRAs through an online search.

- Several people said they contacted only one CRA because they were told that the other two CRAs would be informed of their situation. Others said they contacted all three CRAs themselves because they were not confident that their information would be shared if they only contacted one CRA.

Methods of Contacting CRAs

- Among participants in the focus groups, the most common mode for contacting the CRAs was by telephone. Some of the reasons participants mentioned for calling included "wanting to hear a person's voice" and not having access to a computer.

- Several of the participants also contacted the CRAs online or wrote letters. A few participants mentioned faxing as well, but only as a follow-up to an initial contact through a different channel.

- A few of the participants who contacted the CRAs online said they first tried calling but were directed to the CRA's website to report their identity theft. Others who went online said they did so because they found it difficult to get someone on the telephone. Someone also commented, "Because I'm not the type of person who can hold—I don't have that type of time … I did a lot of my correspondence via e-mail, online."

- A few participants indicated that because they had registered for a paid credit protection service with a particular CRA, that CRA contacted them directly when their identity was stolen.

Satisfaction with CRA Interactions and Perceived Challenges

- When asked in the focus groups to rate their satisfaction with their interactions with the CRAs, most participants indicated that they were either "somewhat satisfied" or "very satisfied." Generally, participants who contacted the CRAs online were most satisfied with their experience. In general, these participants went online to get a fraud alert, and thought that this was fairly easy to do. One participant said, "I found that [going online] for me to be beneficial ... I found that to be easy for me and a quick response. I was pleased with my experience."

- Although the most common method for contacting the CRAs was by telephone, those who did so had mixed experiences. Some of the participants who did this were not satisfied with their experience because they found it very difficult to get a "real person" on the line. These participants commented that they spent a lot of time listening to an automated system or were on hold for a long time.

- In general, most participants were satisfied with the process of getting a fraud alert. However, some complained that while they were on the phone the CRA attempted to sell them various identity theft services, including credit reports or credit monitoring. As a result, some participants said, they ended up buying things that they felt they should have received free of charge.

- Most of the participants who placed a fraud alert on their credit files said that they received some form of confirmation from the CRAs that this was done. Some of the participants who got a fraud alert via telephone said they received paperwork, and those who went online said they received electronic or e-mail confirmation of their fraud alert. Others knew that the fraud alert had been placed because they received a call from a creditor to verify their identity before opening a new account.

- One of the frustrations expressed by focus group participants was that it took longer than expected for them to get their free credit report. This was particularly frustrating because, since they had been the victim of recent identity theft, they wanted to see their report as soon as possible to assess what damage had been done to their credit. One participant said, "My free credit report showed up ... four months later, so the 90-day fraud alert had already expired at that point."

- Some participants complained that even though they were the victims in this situation, when they contacted the CRAs they were in the position of having to prove to the CRA that they were who they said they were. One person said, "I filed a dispute and ... I felt uncomfortable because I actually had to send them a copy of my ID, a copy of my Social Security card, my birth certificate, and all of that information that's already stolen." Another commented that the CRAs made him feel like "prime suspect number one."

- Another source of frustration for participants was the lack of coordination between the various entities that they have to contact when their identity is stolen. For example, several complained that they had to tell the same story and give the same information to the police, the FTC, all of their credit card issuers, their bank, and one or more of the

CRAs. One participant suggested that a system should be set up through which all of these organizations can share the information, so that consumers only have to provide it once.

- A few participants mentioned that not only was their identity stolen but their children's personal information was stolen as well. These participants reported that the CRAs told them that there was nothing that could be done to protect their children's credit until they were at least 18 years old.

Participants' Understanding of FACT Act Rights

In an attempt to gauge participants' understanding of four rights provided by the FACT Act related to identity theft—placing a fraud alert, getting a free copy of a credit report, disputing inaccurate information on a report, and blocking fraudulent information on a report from being disclosed—they were asked to share their opinions of what they think these things are.

In general, before their identity was stolen most participants were not aware of their FACT Act rights. Although the CRAs gave participants information on a specific remedy for their situation, they did not always provide participants with notice of all of the FACT Act rights. Several participants had heard of fraud alerts, but they had very little or no knowledge of the other rights, particularly the right to block fraudulent information from their credit report. Some participants learned about these things during the focus groups. For example, when asked about blocking fraudulent information, one person said, "I saw that on the questionnaire, but I didn't know that was an option."

Of the four FACT Act rights being studied, the right to place a fraud alert was the most commonly exercised by focus group participants. Many also requested a credit report. The other two rights—disputing and blocking information—were much less commonly exercised by participants. For this reason, these latter two rights were also the least understood.

Placing a Fraud Alert

- A majority of the participants understood what it meant to place a fraud alert on their credit file. When asked what it means to place a fraud alert, participants gave responses such as, "if someone tries to open...another credit account, they're going to contact you to see if you really did [want to] open one up."

- In a few cases, participants mistakenly thought that a fraud alert meant that they would receive a call from their credit card company when there were excessive charges on their account. Additionally, in a few instances participants incorrectly referred to a fraud alert as a "block" on their credit report.

Getting a Free Credit Report

- The process of getting a free credit report was generally easy for participants to understand. Most participants seemed to have obtained a free credit report from a CRA at some point in the past. However, some of the participants were unclear about the distinction between the free credit report they received as a result of their identity theft and the annual free credit report to which they have a right regardless of whether they are a victim of identity theft. Participants did not understand these as two different rights that they could exercise with CRAs.

Disputing Inaccurate Information on Your Credit Report

- Many of the participants understood that disputing inaccurate information on their credit file involved writing to the CRAs to let them know that information on their credit report is inaccurate. They also understood that they could ask for the disputed information to be removed if it was found to be incorrect.

- Several people did not understand that if the CRAs investigated the disputed information and decided that it was accurate, it would remain on their credit report; instead, they seemed to mistakenly believe that if they disputed the information it would automatically be removed. This may explain why some participants complained that the CRAs did not update their credit report even though they had disputed information.

- A few of the participants thought that they only should dispute the inaccurate information with individual creditors, who would then make the corrections with the CRAs. One person said, "I would assume the owner has to take the initiative to contact [the creditor] … to have it removed, and then it will be updated in the credit bureau … I had to contact [the creditors] individually … They will in turn contact the credit bureaus."

Blocking Fraudulent Information from Being Disclosed

- Very few participants understood what it means to block fraudulent information on their credit report from being disclosed, and even fewer were aware that this was one of the remedies they could request from the CRAs.

- One of the few participants who understood the right to block fraudulent information stated that you exercise this right when you "don't want the disputed information brought up" when you are applying for credit.

- Some of the people who did not understand this right confused blocking information with disputing its accuracy. For most participants, confusion about what it means to "block fraudulent information" persisted despite the moderator's attempts to explain this to them.

- A few participants also confused the right to block fraudulent information from being disclosed with requesting a fraud alert. This confusion seemed to be because these participants thought a fraud alert would "block" people from seeing their credit report.

Participants' Feedback on the Identity Theft Victim Survey

As noted above, participants in half of the groups were shown a draft of FTC's survey of victims of identity theft. These participants were asked to complete the survey before the focus group discussion, and then were given an opportunity during the discussion to provide feedback on whether questions and response options were clear and easy to understand. The purpose of this portion of the focus groups was to identify comprehension issues on the survey that needed to be addressed before the survey was fielded. In a few cases, participant feedback on the survey—or an analysis of participant responses—directly led to improvements in the survey instrument. Some examples of these improvements as a result of the study are the following:

- During the first round of focus groups in Washington, DC, several participants had difficulty following skip patterns correctly. Many did not follow directions to skip certain questions, and as a result answered questions they should not have. Following this first set of groups, ICF Macro revised the formatting of the survey to make the skip patterns clearer. For example, additional directions were provided at the beginning of some sections of the survey along with the directions after specific questions. These changes were largely successful; participants in the next two sets of focus groups made significantly fewer mistakes when following skip patterns. As a result, the FTC plans to use the revised format in its final survey instrument.

- The survey instrument included definitions of the four FACT Act rights addressed in this project, since the FTC was aware that some respondents would likely not be familiar with these rights. In the first round of focus groups, however, participants had very low comprehension of different FACT Act rights even after taking the survey, which indicated that the definitions had not been effective. The FTC was concerned by this finding because a lack of comprehension of these rights could negatively impact participants' ability to answer survey questions accurately. Therefore, after the first set of groups, ICF Macro revised the survey format to make the definitions more prominent by putting them in boxes and underlining important words and phrases in the definitions. These changes seemed to be effective. While some participants in subsequent groups still had misconceptions about these rights (particularly the ability to block information from being disclosed), comprehension was generally higher than it had been in the first set of groups.

- The survey included a question asking whether respondents had received a notice from the CRAs that summarized their rights. In the version shown to participants in the first set of groups, this question appeared in the first section of the survey, before the individual FACT Act rights were defined. However, as noted above, the focus group discussions showed that participants were generally unaware of their rights as a victim of identity theft. There was some concern, therefore, that respondents would be unable to accurately answer a question about whether they had received a notice of their rights until more specificity about these rights was provided. As a result, this question was moved to a later part of the survey.[2]

- One of the survey items (question 9 on the survey in Appendix A) asked respondents to answer "thinking only of your initial contact with the credit bureau(s)." However, several participants in the focus groups commented that when answering this question they found it difficult to separate how they felt after their initial contact with their general satisfaction. Others who had contacted the CRA more than once said that it was difficult for them to remember how they felt after their initial contact with the CRA. As a result,

---

[2] In the version provided as Appendix A, it appears as question 32.

the FTC is considering revising this question to ask about respondents' overall satisfaction, rather than focusing only on the initial contact.

CONCLUSION

The purpose of the focus groups described in this report was to examine consumers' experiences with CRAs when seeking to exercise one or more of their FACT Act remedies for victims of identity theft. The groups achieved these goals in that they produced a great deal of useful data regarding participants' knowledge of their FACT Act rights, their reasons for contacting the CRAs, and the outcomes of their interactions. Participants also provided a great deal of useful input on the FTC Identity Theft Victim Survey. Some of the most important findings from this consumer research included the following:

- Many of the participants in the focus groups were not fully aware of their FACT Act remedies. When they contacted the CRAs it was not to exercise a specific right, but because of a general expectation that the CRAs could assist them with issues resulting from their identity theft.

- With certain exceptions, most participants were at least somewhat satisfied with their interactions with the CRAs, and found it relatively easy to resolve the issues that resulted from their identity theft. Participants who contacted the CRAs online were generally more satisfied than those who did so by telephone. Participants who called the CRAs often complained that it was difficult to get someone on the phone, because of long waiting periods or difficulty navigating the automated systems.

- Despite the fact that satisfaction was generally high, participants expressed a number of frustrations when interacting with the CRAs, including delays in getting a credit report, a lack of trust on the part of the CRAs, attempts to market products or services, and the lack of coordination between entities such as credit card companies, banks, CRAs, and the police.

- As a result of feedback from participants and an analysis of their responses to the survey, ICF Macro was able to suggest several effective changes to the wording, question order, and formatting of the survey instrument. There was evidence from later groups that these revisions improved respondents' understanding of FACT Act rights, as well as their ability to follow survey directions accurately.

The FTC intends to use the results of this research to inform a mail survey of victims of identity theft nationwide. Our hope is that these findings will be helpful in two ways. First, as noted above, ICF Macro and the FTC were able to use the feedback that participants provided about the survey instrument itself to make revisions to both its structure and content. Second, the knowledge gained through the focus groups about how people think about and discuss their experiences with CRAs will inform the FTC's analysis and interpretation of the survey results. In these ways, the results of these focus groups should improve both the accuracy of the survey data that are collected, and the ability of the FTC to use the survey data to make policy decisions that benefit future victims of identity theft.

Appendix A
Identity Theft Victim Survey

OMB No. 3084-0153
Expires: TBD

Identity Theft Victim Survey
(Questionnaire)

Disclosure of Estimated Burden

The estimated average burden associated with this information collection is 25 minutes per respondent. Burden estimates include the time for reviewing instructions, gathering and maintaining data in the required form, and completing the information collection, but exclude the time for compiling and maintaining business records in the normal course of a respondent's activities. A Federal agency may not conduct or sponsor, and an organization (or a person) is not required to respond to a collection of information, unless it displays a currently valid OMB control number. Comments concerning the accuracy of this burden estimate and suggestions for reducing this burden should be directed to the Office of Information and Regulatory Affairs, Office of Management and Budget, Washington, D.C. 20503, and to Anthony Rodriguez, Federal Trade Commission, 600 Pennsylvania Avenue, N.W., Mail Stop NJ-2 122, Washington, D.C. 20580.

FTC Identity Theft Victim Survey

This survey includes questions relating to your experience as a victim of identity theft and your interactions with one or more credit bureaus. Please respond as accurately and completely as possible.

Section 1: Initial Contact with Credit Bureaus

1. Did you try to contact one or more credit reporting companies (also known as credit bureaus) such as Experian, Equifax, or TransUnion as a result of discovering you were a victim of identity theft? **(Check one answer)**

    _____ Yes
    _____ No → **SKIP to Question 33**
    _____ Don't remember or not sure → **SKIP to Question 33**

    1a. When did you first contact one or more credit bureau(s)?

    _____ Less than one month ago
    _____ 1-6 month(s) ago
    _____ 6-12 months ago
    _____ More than 1 year ago

2. How many credit bureaus did you contact? **(Check one answer)**

    _____ One
    _____ Two
    _____ Three or more
    _____ Don't remember or not sure

3. How did you contact the credit bureau(s)? **(Check as many as apply)**

    _____ Phone
    _____ Mail
    _____ Online
    _____ Other → **Please explain:** _____
    _____ Don't remember or not sure

4. Why did you contact the credit bureau(s)? **(Check as many as apply)**

    _____ Place a fraud alert on your credit report
    _____ Dispute inaccurate information in your credit report
    _____ Block fraudulent information in your credit report
    _____ Get a copy of your credit report
    _____ Get your credit score
    _____ Get information
    _____ Other → **Please explain:** _____
    _____ Don't remember or not sure

5. Did you try to speak with a live person at one or more credit bureaus? **(Check one answer)**

    _____ Yes
    _____ No → **SKIP to Question 9**
    _____ Don't remember or not sure → **SKIP to Question 9**

6. Were you able to speak with a live person? **(Check one answer)**

    _____ Yes
    _____ No → **SKIP to Question 9**
    _____ Don't remember or not sure → **SKIP to Question 9**

7. In general, how easy or difficult was it to reach a live person? **(Check one answer)**

    _____ Very easy
    _____ Somewhat easy
    _____ Somewhat difficult
    _____ Very difficult
    _____ Don't remember or not sure

8. Overall, how useful was the information you received when you spoke to a live person? **(Check one answer)**

    _____ Very useful
    _____ Somewhat useful
    _____ Only slightly useful
    _____ Not at all useful
    _____ Don't remember or not sure

9. Thinking only of your initial contact with the credit bureau(s), how satisfied were you with your experience with the credit bureau(s)? **(Check one answer)**

    _____ Very satisfied
    _____ Somewhat satisfied
    _____ Somewhat dissatisfied
    _____ Very dissatisfied
    _____ Don't know or not sure

    9a. Again, thinking of your initial contact with the credit bureau(s), please tell us why you felt satisfied or dissatisfied with your experience:

    _____

    _____

    _____

    _____

Section 2: Placing a Fraud Alert

DEFINITION: Placing a fraud alert on your credit report requires creditors to follow certain procedures to verify your identity before issuing credit in your name. Often, this means that when a business wants to open a new account in your name, they will first contact you to get your permission to open the account.

10. **Before you contacted a credit bureau,** were you aware that you had a right to request a fraud alert if you believed that you were, or were likely to become, a victim of identity theft? **(Check one answer)**

    _____ Yes
    _____ No
    _____ Don't remember or not sure

11. Did you ask one or more credit bureaus to place a fraud alert on your credit report? **(Check one answer)**

    _____ Yes
    _____ No → **SKIP to Question 20**
    _____ Don't remember or not sure → **SKIP to Question 20**

12. Did you ask for an initial (90 day) fraud alert, an extended (7 year) fraud alert, or both? **(Check one answer)**

    _____ Initial alert only
    _____ Extended alert only
    _____ Both initial and extended alerts
    _____ Don't remember or not sure

13. To the best of your knowledge, was a fraud alert actually placed on your credit report? **(Check one answer)**

    _____ All of the bureaus placed a fraud alert
    _____ Some of the bureaus placed a fraud alert, others did not
    _____ Some of the bureaus placed a fraud alert, I don't know about others
    _____ Don't remember or not sure

14. Overall, how satisfied were you with the experience of placing a fraud alert on your credit report? **(Check one answer)**

   _____ Very satisfied
   _____ Somewhat satisfied
   _____ Somewhat dissatisfied
   _____ Very dissatisfied
   _____ Don't know or not sure

   14a. Please tell us why you felt satisfied or dissatisfied with the experience of placing a fraud alert:

   _____

   _____

   _____

   _____

Section 3: Requesting a Free Credit Report

DEFINITION: When you place a fraud alert on your credit report, you have the right to request a free credit report from each of the credit bureaus. This is separate from your right to an annual free credit report.

NOTE: If you did not answer "Yes" to Question 11, please skip to Question 20 and do not answer this section.

15. **Before you contacted a credit bureau,** were you aware that you had this right to request a free credit report when you place a fraud alert? **(Check one answer)**

   _____ Yes
   _____ No
   _____ Don't remember or not sure

16. Did you request a free copy of your credit report from one or more credit bureaus after you placed a fraud alert?

   _____ Yes
   _____ No → **SKIP to Question 20**
   _____ Don't remember or not sure → **SKIP to Question 20**

17. How did you ask for a free copy of your credit report from the credit bureau(s)? **(Check as many as apply)**

    ____ Call
    ____ Write
    ____ Mail a form
    ____ Go to the website → **If you recall, please identify website:** _____
    ____ Do something else → **Please explain:** _____
    ____ Don't remember or not sure

18. Did you receive a free copy of your credit report from the credit bureau(s)?

    ____ I received a free copy of my credit report from all of the bureaus I contacted
    ____ I received a free copy of my credit report from some of the bureaus I contacted
    ____ I did not receive a copy of my credit report from any of the bureaus I contacted
    ____ Don't remember or not sure

19. Overall, how satisfied were you with your experience in getting your free credit report from the credit bureau(s)? **(Check one answer)**

    ____ Very satisfied
    ____ Somewhat satisfied
    ____ Somewhat dissatisfied
    ____ Very dissatisfied
    ____ Don't know or not sure

19a. Please tell us why you felt satisfied or dissatisfied with your experience in getting a free credit report:

_____

_____

_____

_____

Section 4: Disputing the Accuracy of Information in Your Credit Report

DEFINITION: You have the right to dispute the accuracy of information in your credit report that you believe is inaccurate. The credit bureau will investigate your dispute with the company that reported the disputed information. If the information is, in fact, inaccurate, you have the right to have it corrected or removed.

20.   **Before you contacted a credit bureau,** were you aware that you had this right to dispute the accuracy of information in your credit report? **(Check one answer)**

    ____   Yes
    ____   No
    ____   Don't remember or not sure

21.   Did you dispute the accuracy of any identity theft-related information in your credit report? **(Check one answer)**

    ____   Yes
    ____   No → **SKIP to Question 27**
    ____   Don't remember or not sure → **SKIP to Question 27**

22.   With whom did you file your dispute? **(Check as many as apply)**

    ____   One or more of the credit bureaus (Trans Union, Equifax, or Experian)
    ____   The company that appeared on your credit report with the account or information you were disputing
    ____   Other → **Please explain:** _____
    ____   Don't remember or not sure

23.   What information in your credit report did you dispute? **(Check all that apply)**

    ____   Identification and employment information (name, address, employer, etc.)
    ____   Payment information related to a particular debt (account, amount owed, etc.)
    ____   Creditors you did not authorize to obtain your report
    ____   Other → **Please elaborate:** _____
    ____   Don't remember or not sure

24.   Was the information you disputed removed or corrected? **(Check one answer)**

    ____   Yes
    ____   No → **SKIP to Question 26**
    ____   Don't remember or not sure → **SKIP to Question 26**

25. If you contacted the credit bureau(s) to file your dispute, how many times did you contact the credit bureau(s) before the information you disputed was removed or corrected? **(Check one answer)**

_____ Once
_____ Twice
_____ Three to five times
_____ Six times or more
_____ Don't remember or not sure

26. Overall, how satisfied were you with your experience in disputing information in your credit report? **(Check one answer)**

_____ Very satisfied
_____ Somewhat satisfied
_____ Somewhat dissatisfied
_____ Very dissatisfied
_____ Don't know or not sure

26a. Please tell us why you felt satisfied or dissatisfied with your experience in disputing information in your credit report:

_____

_____

_____

_____

Section 5: Blocking the Release of Fraudulent Information in Your Credit Report

DEFINITION: You have the right to block the release of fraudulent information in your credit report that is the result of identity theft. This right is different than your right to place a fraud alert on your account, or your right to dispute inaccurate information on your credit report.

27. **Before you contacted a credit bureau,** were you aware that you had this right to block fraudulent information in your credit report from being released to others? **(Check one answer)**

_____ Yes
_____ No
_____ Don't remember or not sure

28. Did you ask one or more credit bureaus to block fraudulent identity theft-related information in your credit report from being released? **(Check one answer)**

_____ Yes
_____ No → **SKIP to Question 32**
_____ Don't remember or not sure → **SKIP to Question 32**

29. To the best of your knowledge, did the bureaus you asked actually block fraudulent identity theft-related information in your credit report from being released? **(Check one answer)**

    ____ All of the bureaus blocked the information
    ____ Only some of the bureaus blocked the information
    ____ None of the bureaus blocked the information → **SKIP to Question 31**
    ____ Don't remember or not sure → **SKIP to Question 31**

30. How long did it typically take the credit bureaus to block information in your credit report? **(Check one answer)**

    ____ One day (24 hours)
    ____ 2 - 7 days
    ____ More than 7 days
    ____ Don't remember or not sure

31. Overall, how satisfied were you with your experience in blocking fraudulent information in your credit report? **(Check one answer)**

    ____ Very satisfied
    ____ Somewhat satisfied
    ____ Somewhat dissatisfied
    ____ Very dissatisfied
    ____ Don't know or not sure

    31a. Please tell us why you felt satisfied or dissatisfied with your experience in blocking information in your credit report:

    _____

    _____

    _____

    _____

Section 6: Additional Questions

32. By law, credit bureaus must give you a notice that summarizes your rights as a victim of identity theft. Did you receive such a "notice of rights" from the credit bureau(s) you contacted? **(Check one answer)**

    ____ I received a "notice of rights" from all of the credit bureaus I contacted
    ____ I received a "notice of rights" from some of the credit bureaus I contacted
    ____ I did not receive a "notice of rights" from any of the credit bureaus I contacted
    ____ I don't remember or not sure

33.   Feel free to include additional comments below:

_____

_____

_____

_____

Thank you for completing this survey.
Please complete the Pretest Questionnaire on the next page.

PRETEST QUESTIONNAIRE

1. How difficult was it for you to complete this survey?
   - Not difficult at all
   - Somewhat difficult
   - Very difficult
   - Impossible, I was not able to complete this survey.

   Please explain the answer you selected for Question 1:

   _____

   _____

   _____

   _____

2. Were any of the questions difficult to understand or answer? If so, please tell us which questions you found difficult and why.

   _____

   _____

   _____

   _____

3. Were there any terms or phrases used in this survey that you had difficulty understanding? If so, please explain below.

   _____

   _____

   _____

   _____

5. Please provide any other comments you have about this survey.

   _____

   _____

   _____

   _____

Appendix B
Focus Group Moderator Guides

Federal Trade Commission
Identity Theft Victims
Focus Group Moderator Guide

I.   Introduction (10 minutes)

Hello, and thank you for taking the time to join us this evening. My name is *(name)*, and I am going to be moderating our discussion tonight. I work for ICF Macro, a research firm located near Washington, D.C.

Purpose

My company has been hired by the Federal Trade Commission (FTC) to conduct a set of focus groups with people whose identity has been stolen and have contacted one or more of the national credit bureaus as a result. The credit bureaus, also known as consumer reporting agencies (CRAs) are Experian, Equifax and TransUnion. The FTC is using focus groups like this one across the country to gain a better understanding of consumers' experiences interacting with credit bureaus after their identity was stolen. The information you provide will help to guide the FTC's efforts to educate consumers and regulate the credit bureaus.

Ground Rules

To make our discussion productive and run smoothly for everyone, there are some basic ground rules we will need to follow. [*Post rules on flip chart in the room for reference if needed*].

- Everyone's input is important. *I will work hard to make sure everyone has the chance to speak.*
- Please speak one at a time and avoid side conversations.
- Stay focused on the question. To get to all the topics of the discussion, I may need to cut a discussion short to move things along more quickly. Please don't take this personally.
- This session is being audio taped and videotaped.
- There are people from the Federal Trade Commission behind the glass observing our discussion.
- Everything that is said in this session will be held confidential; your name will never be linked to anything that you say in any future reports.
- Please turn pagers and cells phones off or to silent.

My role here is to guide the discussion and listen to your honest opinions about your experiences interacting with the credit bureaus, but keep in mind that I am not an expert on the topic.

Do you have any questions before we get started?

Now, I would like to give everyone a chance to introduce themselves. Please tell us your first name only, and briefly describe how your identity was stolen if you know how (e.g. Your information was stolen from an institution you do business with, your wallet was stolen, etc.). If your identity has been stolen more than once, please talk about the most recent incident.

II. Opening Questions (5 minutes)

1. What did you do when you found out your identity had been stolen?

2. Had you known in advance what you should do if your identity is stolen? If so, where did you get that information? (e.g., from a friend or family member, the internet, etc.)

III. Extent and nature of contacts with the credit bureaus (30 minutes)

3. How long after your identity had been stolen did you contact a credit bureau?

4. How many credit bureaus did you contact?
   a. Why did you contact more than one credit bureau?

5. How did you contact the credit bureau(s)?
   a. Why did you contact the credit bureaus in the way(s) that you did?

   Get responses from a few participants then ask for a show of hands of those who contacted the credit bureau(s) by phone, mail, internet, email, or any other method. Make clear to participants that they can choose more than one answer, if appropriate.

6. Why did you contact a credit bureau? Were you told to by someone, or was it something you thought to do on your own?

7. What were you hoping to accomplish by calling a credit bureau? *Probe to see what, if any, specific actions participants wanted the credit bureau to take—or what they thought the credit bureau could accomplish.*

8. Did you know specifically what you wanted from the credit bureau before you called? If not, how did you learn what the credit bureaus could do for you? Did they tell you?

Show participants the following list, which will have been written on a flip chart before the group begins:
   1) Place a "fraud alert"
   2) Get a free copy of your credit report
   3) Dispute inaccurate information on your credit report
   4) Block fraudulent information on your credit report from being disclosed

9. This list shows four different reasons that you could have contacted the credit bureaus. *Point to #1 on the list.* Could someone explain to me what this first item means? In other

words, if you called the credit bureau to place a "fraud alert," what were you asking them to do?

    a. Is there anyone who thinks this means something different?

    b. *Once you have gotten as many interpretations as possible, describe to participants the actual meaning of that phrase.* How many of you would have known before this discussion what this phrase meant?

Repeat Q7 for each of the four actions on the list.

10. I'd like everyone to indicate, by a show of hands, whether they asked the credit bureau to do each of these things. You can raise your hand for as many as apply to you—you don't have to pick just one. *Get a show of hands for each of the four.*

11. By law, as a victim of identity theft you have the right to do all four of the things listed here (*point to flip chart*). The credit bureaus are required to inform you of these rights when you contact them to tell them that your identity has been stolen. Did the credit bureau(s) you contacted inform you of these rights?

    a. Did they do so in writing?

IV.   Outcome of contacts with credit bureaus (25 minutes)

12. Describe the first time you contacted the credit bureau(s).

    a. Did you try to reach a "real person?"

    b. If so, were you successful in reaching a "real person?"

13. What was the outcome of your first interaction with the credit bureau?

14. Did you get what you wanted from the credit bureau as a result of that initial interaction?

(For people who got what they wanted)

    a. Please explain.

    b. How long did it take to get the result you wanted?

    c. How did you know the credit bureau had done what you wanted/requested (e.g., placing a fraud alert on your account)?

(For people who did not get what they wanted)

    a. Please explain.

    b. How did you find out that you had not gotten what you wanted, or that the credit bureau didn't do what you requested? Do you know that it didn't happen, or are you not sure?

    c. Why do you think the credit bureau didn't do what you wanted? For example, did the credit bureau(s) misunderstand your request? Did they ignore your request?

15. For those of you who did not initially get what you wanted from the credit bureau, what did you do then? Did you contact the credit bureau again? What happened when you continued to contact the credit bureaus?
    a. Did you ever get the outcome you wanted?
    b. How difficult was it to get the outcome you wanted?
    c. In all, about how many times did you have to contact the credit bureau to get the desired outcome?
    d. About how long did it take?

V. Wrap-up (10 minutes)

Show participants the following list, which will have been written on a flip chart before the group begins.
Very satisfied
Somewhat satisfied
Somewhat dissatisfied
Very dissatisfied

16. Using this scale, how satisfied were you with your overall experience with the credit bureau(s)? *Ask for a show of hands for each rating. If participants indicate that they are dissatisfied and have not already discussed why, ask them to explain their answer.*

17. What could have made your experience with the credit bureaus more successful?
    a. What should the credit bureau(s) have done differently?
    b. Is there anything that you should have done differently?

False Close (10 minutes)

At this point, let participants know that you are going to see if the observers for FTC have any final questions they want to ask. FTC staff will then have the opportunity to suggest follow-up questions or ask the moderator to go back to get clarification on earlier participant comments. The remainder of the session will be focused on this follow-up.

Closure and Thank You

Thank you very much for taking the time to participate in this discussion. Your input has been helpful. To show our appreciation for your participation, someone will have a check for you on the way out. You'll be asked to sign for that.

We also have some information for you about resolving identity theft. I'll distribute these to you now so you can take them with you. Thanks again and have a good evening.

Federal Trade Commission
Identity Theft Victims
Focus Group Moderator Guide II

I. Introduction and Survey (30 minutes)

Hello, and thank you for taking the time to join us this evening. My name is Shauna Clarke, and I am going to be moderating our discussion tonight. I work for ICF Macro, a research firm located near Washington, D.C.

Purpose

My company has been hired by the Federal Trade Commission (FTC) to conduct a set of focus groups with people whose identity has been stolen and have contacted one or more of the national credit bureaus as a result. The credit bureaus, also known as consumer reporting agencies (CRAs) are Experian, Equifax and TransUnion. The FTC is using focus groups like this one across the country to gain a better understanding of consumers' experiences interacting with credit bureaus after their identity was stolen. The information you provide will help to guide the FTC's efforts to educate consumers and regulate the credit bureaus.

For the next half hour, we are going to ask you to complete a written survey. This is a draft version of a survey that will eventually be mailed to identity theft victims across the country. At 8:30, we will get together for a discussion that I will lead. The purpose of that discussion will be both to talk about your experiences with the credit bureaus and to get your feedback on various aspects of the survey you completed.

Instructions for the Survey

- Please complete the survey as you would if you were at home.
- You will have 20 minutes to complete your survey.
- Please write only your first name on the survey.
- If you encounter anything in the survey that you find confusing or unclear (such as a word you don't understand, or a question you are not sure how to answer), please write down what you find confusing—or at the very least, mark the question so you can bring it up later during our discussion.
- When you are finished, please bring your survey to the front desk [*or other location, depending on the layout of the facility*].

After everyone has completed the survey, collect them and record responses to key questions. Make a note of any questions with interesting results for the group discussion.

Ground Rules for the Discussion (5 minutes)

Now we will begin the discussion part of the focus group. Again, this discussion will have two purposes: to learn more about your experiences interacting with the credit reporting agencies and to get your feedback on various aspects of the survey you just completed.

To make sure that this discussion is productive and runs smoothly for everyone, there are some basic ground rules we will need to follow.

- Everyone's input is important. *I will work hard to make sure everyone has the chance to speak.*
- Please speak one at a time and avoid side conversations.
- Stay focused on the question. To get to all the topics of the discussion, I may need to cut a discussion short to move things along more quickly. Please don't take this personally.
- This session is being audiotaped and videotaped.
- There are people from the Federal Trade Commission behind the glass observing our discussion.
- Everything that is said in this session will be held confidential; your name will never be linked to anything that you say in any future reports.
- Please turn pagers and cells phones off or to silent.

My role here is to guide the discussion and listen to your honest opinions about your experiences interacting with the credit bureaus, but keep in mind that I am not an expert on the topic.

Do you have any questions before we get started?

Now, I would like to give everyone a chance to introduce themselves. Please tell us your first name only, and briefly describe how your identity was stolen if you know how (e.g. Your information was stolen from an institution you do business with, your wallet was stolen, etc.). If your identity has been stolen more than once, please talk about the most recent incident.

II.   Nature of contacts with the credit bureaus (25 minutes)

1. All of you eventually contacted a credit bureau after your identity was stolen—is that correct? Why did you contact a credit bureau? Were you told to by someone, or was it something you thought to do on your own?

2. What were you hoping to accomplish by calling a credit bureau? *Probe to see what, if any, specific actions participants wanted the credit bureau to take—or what they thought the credit bureau could accomplish.*

3. Did you know specifically what you wanted from the credit bureau before you called? If not, how did you learn what the credit bureaus could do for you? Did they tell you?

Show participants the following list, which will have been written on a flip chart before the group begins:
1) *Place a "fraud alert"*
2) *Get a free copy of your credit report*
3) *Dispute inaccurate information on your credit report*
4) *Block fraudulent information on your credit report from being disclosed*

4. This list shows four different reasons that you could have contacted the credit bureaus. *Point to #1 on the list.* Could someone explain to me what this first item means? In other words, if you called the credit bureau to place a "fraud alert," what were you asking them to do?
   a. Is there anyone who thinks this means something different?
   b. *Once you have gotten as many interpretations as possible, describe to participants the actual meaning of that phrase.* How many of you understood what this phrase meant when you were completing the survey?

Repeat Q4 for each of the four actions on the list.

5. I'd like everyone to indicate, by a show of hands, whether they asked the credit bureau to do each of these things. You can raise your hand for as many as apply to you—you don't have to pick just one. *Get a show of hands for each of the four.* **As you count off each one, say the participants' names so that the observer can cross-check their answers with their responses to the survey.**

III. Outcome of contacts with credit bureaus (20 minutes)

6. Did you get what you wanted from the credit bureau as a result of your first interaction with them (that is, your first call, first e-mail, first letter)?

   (For people who got what they wanted)
   a. Please explain.
   b. How long did it take to get the result you wanted?
   c. How did you know the credit bureau had done what you wanted/requested (e.g., placing a fraud alert on your account)?

   (For people who did not get what they wanted)
   a. Please explain.
   b. How did you find out that you had not gotten what you wanted, or that the credit bureau didn't do what you requested? Do you know that it didn't happen, or are you not sure?
   c. Why do you think the credit bureau didn't do what you wanted? For example, did the credit bureau(s) misunderstand your request? Did they ignore your request?

7. For those of you who did not initially get what you wanted from the credit bureau, what did you do then? Did you contact the credit bureau again? What happened when you continued to contact the credit bureaus?
   a. Did you ever get the outcome you wanted?
   b. How difficult was it to get the outcome you wanted?
   c. In all, about how many times did you have to contact the credit bureau to get the desired outcome?
   d. About how long did it take?

IV. Review of Completed Surveys (20 minutes)

At this point, I'd like to hand back the surveys that you completed earlier this evening so that we can talk about them. Again, this is a draft version of a survey that will eventually be mailed to identity theft victims across the country—so we are interested in getting your feedback about any portions of the survey that might be confusing or unclear. Please do not write on these surveys, or change any of your answers. If you decide during the course of our discussion that you want to change any of your answers, bring it up in the discussion but leave the written form as is. *Return the completed surveys to each participant.*

8. Did anyone have any difficulty answering questions in the first section (questions 1-9a)?
   a. Were the instructions in that section clear?

9. Let's now look at question 7. When you answered this question, did you fully understand all of these options—or did you not know what one or more of the options meant?
   a. Now that we have talked more about the various reasons that you might have contacted a credit bureau, is there anyone here who would want to change their answer to question 4? If so, why?

10. Did anyone have any difficulty answering question 9? If so, why?
   a. The directions for question 9 specifically state that you are only supposed to consider your initial contact with the credit bureau when answering this question. Was that direction clear to everyone? Is there anyone here who actually answered this question based on other contacts they had with their credit bureau other than the first one?
   b. Imagine that the question would have asked you to rate your satisfaction based on ALL your interactions with the credit bureau, not just the first. Would your answer have been different? *Probe to see how many people would have answered differently.*

11. Now let's move on through the survey. Section 2 of the survey deals with fraud alerts. Did anyone have any difficulty answering any of the questions in Section 2 (questions 10-14a)? If so, why?

12. How did you answer question 13? Was it clear to you which was the correct response for you?
    a. How do you know whether or not the bureaus placed a fraud alert on your credit report?
    b. On question 13, the first response reads "all of the bureaus placed a fraud alert." When you read this, did you think this meant all of the bureaus placed an alert, or all of the bureaus that you contacted placed an alert? *Probe to see if there was any disagreement between participants on this question.*

13. Section 3 of the survey deals with requesting a free credit report. Did anyone have any difficulty answering any of the questions in Section 3 (questions 15-19a)? If so, why?

14. The questions in Section 4 relate to disputing information on your credit report. Did anyone have any difficulty answering any of the questions in Section 4 (questions 20-26a)? If so, why?

15. How did you answer question 24? Was it clear to you which was the correct response for you?
    a. If you disputed information on your credit report, how do you know whether or not the bureaus removed or corrected the information?

16. The questions in Section 5 relate to blocking fraudulent information from being released. Did anyone have any difficulty answering any of the questions in Section 5 (questions 27-32)?

17. How did you answer question 29? Was it clear to you which was the correct response for you?
    a. If you tried to block information on your credit report from being released, how do you know whether or not the bureaus blocked the information?

V.   Other Survey Feedback (5 minutes)

18. Are there aspects of your experiences with the credit bureau(s) that were not covered by this survey that you feel that the FTC should know about?

19. Again, this survey will eventually be administered across the country by mail. However, the FTC anticipates that some people may be reluctant to complete and return it. What suggestions do you have for how the FTC could encourage people to complete it?

VI.　Wrap-Up (5 minutes)

20. What could have made your experience with the credit bureaus more successful?
    a. What should the credit bureau(s) have done differently?
    b. Is there anything that you should have done differently?

False Close (10 minutes)

At this point, let participants know that you are going to see if the observers for FTC have any final questions they want to ask. FTC staff will then have the opportunity to suggest follow-up questions or ask the moderator to go back to get clarification on earlier participant comments. The remainder of the session will be focused on this follow-up.

Closure and Thank You

Thank you very much for taking the time to participate in this discussion. Your input has been helpful. To show our appreciation for your participation, someone will have a check for you on the way out. You'll be asked to sign for that.

Please pass the surveys down to me. *Be sure to collect completed surveys from all participants.* We also have some information for you about resolving identity theft. I'll distribute these to you now so you can take them with you. Thanks again and have a good evening.

Appendix C
Focus Group Recruitment Letter

Bureau of Consumer Protection
Division of Privacy and Identity Protection

September 28, 2009

Consumer Name
Address
City, State and Zip

Dear _____,

    The Federal Trade Commission (FTC), with the assistance of an outside research organization, is conducting focus groups with victims of identity theft. We are contacting you to request your participation in one of the focus groups in your area. Information we receive in these focus group discussions will assist us in gaining a better understanding of consumers' experiences interacting with credit bureaus after their identity was stolen. The information you provide will help to guide the FTC's efforts to educate consumers and regulate the credit bureaus. We are not selling anything, and you will not be solicited to purchase anything as a result of your participation in this survey.

    Our records show that you have filed a complaint with the FTC relating to identity theft. While the FTC will not be able to use information you share in the focus groups to investigate your individual complaint, we will use the information to identify trends and patterns that emerge from all of the participants in the focus groups. Your participation in these focus groups is completely voluntary, but extremely important to help us get an accurate understanding of the experiences of identity theft victims such as yourself. You will not be asked for personal information and your responses will be maintained without any information to identify you. You will receive $75 as compensation for your time.

    If you are interested in participating, please contact Focus Pointe Global's recruiting department at 1-800-220-3730 and tell them you would like to participate in group **#37296CG.** Space is limited so please contact Focus Pointe Global as soon as possible to be scheduled for the focus group

    If you have any questions regarding this letter, please feel free to contact Cheryl Thomas, paralegal, in the FTC's Division of Privacy and Identity Protection via email at idtheftsurvey@ftc.gov or by phone at (202) 326-2252.

Thank you for your help in this matter.

                  Sincerely,

                  Rebecca E. Kuehn
                  Assistant Director
                  Division of Privacy and Identity Protection

C-2

Appendix D
Participant Recruitment Screener

Federal Trade Commission
Identity Theft Focus Groups
Participant Screener

Purpose:
- To recruit volunteers for focus groups with individuals who have experienced identity theft
- Recruit participants for one 2-hour focus group (stipend = $75)
- Recruit participants for one 90-minute focus group (stipend = $75)
- Recruit 13 participants for a total of 10 to show in each group

Hello, my name is _____ and I'm calling on behalf of the Federal Trade Commission. The Federal Trade Commission is sponsoring a series of focus groups involving people whose identity has been stolen. We received your name from the Federal Trade Commission because you filed a complaint with them related to identity theft. You may have received a letter about this study in the past week or so.

The purpose of these focus groups is to gain a better understanding of consumers' experiences with identity theft, and the information you provide will help to guide the FTC's efforts to educate consumers and regulate the credit bureaus.

The focus group in your area will take place on (Date, at 6:00 and 8:30) and will last about (90 minutes/2 hours). If you participate in this group you will be compensated ($75) for your time.

Do you think you will be willing and able to participate?
_____ Yes **(Continue)**
_____ No **(Terminate)**

Your answers to the following questions are strictly confidential. We will never release your identity to anyone other than the organization conducting this study. You are not required to answer any of these questions. You may end this interview at anytime if you wish.

All of the people contacted should qualify for the focus groups from a preexisting list.

1. *How long ago was your identity stolen? (If you have experienced more than once incidence of identity theft, please respond based on the most recent incident.)* (Quota: No more than 4 in each group should respond (c))
   _____ a) Less than 3 months ago
   _____ b) 3-6 months ago
   _____ c) 6-12 months ago

2. *After you learned that your identity had been stolen, did you contact one or more of the national credit bureaus? (These bureaus include Experian, Equifax, and TransUnion.)*

_____ Yes

_____ No **(Terminate)**

3. *What is your gender?* (Quota: At least 4 participants of each gender in each group)
   _____ a) Male
   _____ b) Female

4. *What is your age?* (Quota: At least 3 participants of each category in each group)
   _____ a) 18-34
   _____ b) 35-54
   _____ c) 55 or older

(Quota: No more than 8 participants in each group can respond (b) on question 5 and (e) on question 6.)

5. *Which of the following categories best describe your race?*
   _____ a) Hispanic or Latino
   _____ b) Not Hispanic or Latino

6. *Please select one or more of the following categories that best describes your ethnicity.*
   _____ a) American Indian or Alaska Native
   _____ b) Asian
   _____ c) Black or African American
   _____ d) Native Hawaiian or Other Pacific Islander
   _____ e) White

7. *What it the highest level of education you have completed?* (Quota: At least 4 participants in each group respond (a) or (b))
   _____ a) Less than high school
   _____ b) High school graduate or GED
   _____ c) Some college
   _____ d) College graduate or higher

8. *Which of the following statement best applies to you?* (Quota: At least 6 participants in each group respond (b) or (c))
   _____ a) I was satisfied with how the credit bureaus worked with me to resolve my identity theft.
   _____ b) I was not satisfied with how the credit bureaus worked with me to resolve my identity theft.
   _____ c) I am still in the process of working with the credit bureaus to resolve my identity theft.

*Thank you for answering my questions. The focus group will take place on **(Date, at 6:00/8:30)** at (focus group facility location). We will provide you with a ($75) stipend for participating in the focus group, as well as refreshments.*

We will send you a confirmation in the mail. Since we are only inviting a few people, it is very important that you notify us as soon as possible if you are unable to attend.

Thank you for your time.